Your Christ

M...
n...
#... designed to help you make the most of such moments whenever you can. This booklet should be small enough to fit in a bag or a pocket so that you can carry it with you and use wherever you are over the Christmas period – at home, on the move, visiting family and friends.

There are 13 reflections in total. To start with there is one for each of the four weeks before Christmas – the season of Advent. Then there is one for each day from Christmas Eve (24th December) to New Year's Day (1st January).

Each reflection contains:
- A theme
- A picture
- An introduction, focusing on an aspect of the festive season
- An exploration of the themes within the Christmas story
- An invitation to you to consider a particular question, action or attitude
- A very short passage from the Bible to explore and ponder.

At the end of the booklet you will find suggested next steps for your journey – this Christmas, and beyond.

Steps on the Journey

Pray
*Prayer is where
the journey begins*

Practise
*3 important steps on
your Christmas journey*

Equip
3 gifts to take on your Christmas journey

Begin
3 things to help you move on in your Christmas journey

Going further
Next steps for your journey this Christmas and beyond

Advent Week 1

Listening

The weeks before Christmas can be busy and noisy. There are moments and places where silence is a gift, like the quiet of a city street or country lane after a fall of snow.

Prayer does not begin, or end, with words. It starts in stillness and finds its fullest expression in silence.

As we are silent, we learn to listen. We discover how to pay attention to what is going on within us and to what is happening around us.

Listening to your heart and to the world begins to enable you to listen to God. You might only hear him faintly, but as you do so you can catch his whisper of love.

> Now there was a great wind, but the Lord was not in the wind; and after the wind an earthquake, but the Lord was not in the earthquake; and after the earthquake a fire, but the Lord was not in the fire; and after the fire a sound of sheer silence.

Elijah, the prophet, was fed up and angry. He walked 400 miles complaining to God that everyone else had given up and abandoned him. God waited until Elijah had finished and was quiet and then God spoke; not in a violent wind, or an earthquake or a raging fire, but in a breath of silence.

Where this week can you find a moment of silence? *As you pray this week, pray with open ears, to listen to God's whisper.*

READ 1 Kings 19.1-12

Watching

The lights of Christmas – in shops, on streets and in our homes – are bold, beautiful, colourful and often dazzling. Occasionally one small light catches our eye – perhaps a candle's flickering flame – and we see something new.

Prayer is taking time to look. It's pausing long enough to see the goodness, wonder and beauty around you.

Prayer is refusing to rush out the door in the morning before stopping to see the good things that shape and fill your life.

> *Then Jacob woke from his sleep and said, 'Surely the Lord is in this place— and I did not know it!' And he was afraid, and said, 'How awesome is this place! This is none other than the house of God, and this is the gate of heaven.*

It's making time to see, what might otherwise remain unnoticed, the signs of God's presence in the world and in the people you encounter today, and in your own life. The signs are there and you will see them if you open your eyes.

Jacob, running away from home, stops to sleep in the desert and dreams a colourful dream. He sees a ladder stretched from earth to heaven, with angels going up and coming down. He wakes and knows that God is in this place.

Where this week can you recognise the presence of God? As you pray this week, pray with open eyes, to see God's presence around you.

READ Genesis 28.10-17

9

Waiting

For a child, waiting for Christmas is part of the excitement. Many still enjoy the Advent calendar countdown, whether or not accompanied by chocolate!

Prayer is not an instant fix with immediate answers to your personal requests. It is much more like a kind of waiting, perhaps even a longing.

As we listen, watch and learn to wait, we become aware of our own deeper needs and, just as importantly, the longings and cries of others.

Prayer is not giving God a shopping list. It is putting into God's hands things that worry us or issues with which we struggle; it is waiting for God's answer and help. When we pray we share the cries of those near us, and far from us, who wait for healing, or love or justice.

> *Hannah was praying silently; only her lips moved, but her voice was not heard; therefore Eli thought she was drunk.... Hannah answered, 'No, my lord, I am a woman deeply troubled; I have drunk neither wine nor strong drink, but I have been pouring out my soul before the Lord.'*

Hannah is broken-hearted because she has no child, and is made fun of by others. She comes to the temple and prays, her grieving lips moving silently. She waits and God hears her.

In what ways this week are you being asked to wait? *As you pray this week, pray with an open heart, to wait for God's love.*

READ 1 Samuel 1.9-17

Welcoming

Christmas wouldn't be Christmas without presents nor the moment of excitement as gifts are unwrapped or stockings emptied. It takes a bit of time, but we can't enjoy the gift until we've done it.

Prayer is a kind of unwrapping. As we pray we begin to receive a gift from God, gradually and gently, and it is every bit as exciting as opening the very best of Christmas presents.

Prayer is so much more than telling God what I need or what I would like him to do. Rather, it is allowing God to show me what he is longing to give me and what his love is already doing in the world. Prayer is discovery and welcome, and that's what makes it wonderful.

> And Mary said, 'My soul magnifies the Lord, and my spirit rejoices in God my Saviour, for he has looked with favour on the lowliness of his servant. Surely, from now on all generations will call me blessed.'

Mary visits her cousin Elizabeth. Elizabeth's unborn baby jumps for joy, and Mary sings a song of wonder for all that God is doing in the world. Mary begins to see what the gift she is carrying, the baby who will be born and called Jesus, will bring.

Mary welcomes the gift of God's love that will turn the world upside down.

How might you, in this week, discover and welcome more of God's gift to you?

As you pray this week, pray with open hands, to receive what God gives.

READ Luke 1.46-55

Stop

At some point on Christmas Eve we all have to stop. There's a moment when no more last-minute preparation can be done.

Your Christmas journey begins by stopping. It's true with our personal journeys too: moments of breakthrough and discovery come as we stop.

Sometimes we stop because we reach the end of our own resources. At other times it's because we discover the gift of silence and stillness. Or maybe we simply realise that there's too much else getting in the way.

Whatever the reason, stopping is a gift and it's often a new beginning. In fact there's very little we can do to grow personally and spiritually unless we first make the choice to stop. It's the place of prayer and it's where we meet with God.

> While they were there the time came for her to deliver her child. And she gave birth to her firstborn son and wrapped him in bands of cloth, and laid him in a manger, because there was no place for them in the inn.

Mary and Joseph arrive in Bethlehem after a long journey from Nazareth. They are exhausted. Mary is in the last stages of pregnancy, and there is no room in the lodging houses. All they can do is stop where they are offered a space. That night – this night – the gift that is Jesus Christ is born.

How today can you find space to stop, even for five minutes?

READ Luke 2.1-7

Celebrate

Celebration is the heart of Christmas Day. It's a feast day to be shared generously with friends, family and guests.

Your Christmas journey is not travelled alone. It is filled with celebration, feasting and shaped by the love and lives of those who travel with you.

It's pretty clear that we learn about ourselves not in isolation but in relationship. To be loved and to belong is a wonderful gift; it's that gift that helps us discover who we are and find the freedom to grow.

Christmas Day is a day of celebration. God is with us.

In the mess and the muddle, as well as the wonder and the joy. You are loved. You belong. Whoever you are and whatever your situation, God is with you.

> Suddenly there was with the angel a multitude of the heavenly host, praising God and saying, 'Glory to God in the highest heaven, and on earth peace among those whom he favours!'

Shepherds, alone on a hillside, were joined by a choir of angels who lit up the skies with their song of celebration and invited the shepherds – and us – to join in.

Who will you choose to celebrate with today? *Who will be a gift to you?*

READ Luke 2.8-14

Boxing Day

Give

Boxing Day is a day to remember others and to give. Boxes of gifts were traditionally given to those in need or simply to say thank you.

Today is the Feast of Stephen on which Good King Wenceslas waded through a snowstorm to offer help to those in need.

Your Christmas journey is a gift that finds life and direction as you discover the joy of giving. Gifts come in all different shapes and sizes. A small present can bring as much delight as one that is big and expensive. The thought and love behind it is often the real gift.

> 'Let us go now to Bethlehem and see this thing that has taken place, which the Lord has made known to us.' So they went with haste and found Mary and Joseph, and the child lying in the manger.

There is also great joy to be discovered in generous, unconditional giving. As we give we can be surprised by the delight that we ourselves experience – and that is itself a wonderful gift. God gives constantly. Fully and freely. No strings attached. Love, forgiveness, peace – and life to be enjoyed to the full.

The shepherds made the choice to go to the stable and see Jesus, and to give him all they had – their curiosity, their story and their love. They were filled with joy.

What can you do for someone else today? Let it be a gift to them and a gift to you.

READ Luke 2.15-20

Faith

Many people will make time today to walk, perhaps out in the countryside, or with the family in the park, or down the high street to visit the sales.

The shepherds came to visit the stable from a nearby hillside, probably a walk of less than an hour. The wise men travelled for weeks from a distance away.

The shepherds heard and saw a loud, unmistakeable choir of angels. The Magi (or wise men) were guided by the flickering light of a star in the night sky. It was faith that made the shepherds and the Magi step out on their journeys to find Jesus. It's faith that enables you to walk your Christmas journey.

> They set out; and there, ahead of them, went the star that they had seen at its rising, until it stopped over the place where the child was. When they saw that the star had stopped, they were overwhelmed with joy.

Faith is not a leap in the dark, it is a choice to follow a light, however bright or flickering it is. Christian faith is choosing a life that is shaped by the story and person of Jesus Christ. For some, this is an easy and speedy choice, perhaps one that takes us by surprise. For others, the choice takes times and comes after a long journey of searching. However it comes to you, faith is the gift that helps us take another step to God.

How might faith shape the choices you make today?

READ Matthew 2.1-12

21

Hope

Christmas is for many a time to escape. Life is busy and stressful, the world is troubled. For some, family life itself has its difficult moments.

At the heart of our Christmas celebrations is the amazing truth that in all the pain, the struggles and even times of terror, God is with us.

As the wise men began their journey home, Herod ordered the slaughter of children in Bethlehem under two. Unimaginable horror. This is the world into which Jesus was born. This is the world in which we can say with quiet certainty, God is with us.

Your Christmas journey is not an escape from life's harsh realities but an opportunity to discover that even in the darkest places there is hope. Like faith, it's a gift you can choose to take hold of. The life of Jesus offers a new perspective. Darkness will not overcome the light.

> *In him was life, and the life was the light of all people. The light shines in the darkness, and the darkness did not overcome it.*

As we engage day by day with the words and the life of Jesus, we find that it is hope not despair that shapes the way we see the world. As we see differently we begin to live differently and living differently we can change the world.

How might hope shape your perspective today?

READ Matthew 2.16-18

AND John 1.1-5

Love

"If you look for it, I've got a sneaky feeling you'll find that love actually is all around." A brilliant line from the much-loved Christmas film *Love Actually*.

There's a third gift to take on your Christmas journey. Faith, hope and ... love. It's a gift that unwraps as we both receive it and give it. We can find it in surprising places and can give it in unexpected ways.

Mary, Joseph and Jesus flee as refugees to Egypt. As vulnerable foreigners in that country they find welcome and shelter, for what might have been some years.

We live in a time in history where there are almost certainly more refugees than ever before. Love is not just feeling bad about it, love is doing something about it.

> *Then Joseph got up, took the child and his mother by night, and went to Egypt, and remained there until the death of Herod.*

The love we see in the birth and life of Jesus is the love at the heart of God. It is always reaching out, always welcoming, serving, challenging and healing. God's love feels deeply and acts generously. It's seen in the manger and on the cross.

It is that love, more than anything, that is the gift that will bring life to your Christmas journey.

How might love shape your actions today?

READ Matthew 2.13-15

Let Go

The end of the year is approaching. The remains from Christmas celebrations are probably still lying around. It's a good time for a clear out.

There are times in life where we need to let go in order to receive. Sometimes it's just a matter of practicality: our hands are too full of stuff in order to take hold of the gift someone is wanting to give us.

At other times so many things that fill our minds or trouble our hearts that we just don't have the capacity to take on anything new – even when it is potentially life-giving or life-saving.

Your Christmas journey is no exception. It's a journey that promises life and to grasp it fully will mean letting go of things that stop us moving forward.

Pride or fear can prevent us from stepping out on the journey, or it might be shame or hurts that we have carried for many

> Jesus said, 'Come to me, all you that are weary and are carrying heavy burdens, and I will give you rest. Take my yoke upon you, and learn from me; for I am gentle and humble in heart, and you will find rest for your souls. For my yoke is easy, and my burden is light.'

years. Letting go is not always simple; it might, for example, mean taking time to put something right. Jesus invites us to let go of the burdens we carry and receive the gifts of rest, forgiveness and peace that he offers.

What can you let go of today, in order to move on?

READ Matthew 11.28-30

Choose

New Year's Eve is a great day to think about the year ahead and the resolutions you might choose to make.

It's worth pausing today and asking a simple question of any New Year's resolutions you might be thinking of making. The question is this. In what ways will this bring life to me and to others?

When God's people were setting out on a journey several centuries before the birth of Jesus, God offered them a choice. The invitation ends with the words: 'therefore choose life'.

Your Christmas journey is a daily invitation to choose life. That's what makes it so exciting.

> *Jesus said, 'The thief comes only to steal and kill and destroy. I came that they may have life, and have it abundantly.'*

Choosing life is choosing to live by faith, hope and love – letting those life-changing gifts shape what you are and what you do.

Choosing life is choosing to remember that you're not on your own; knowing that you journey with others, and with the friendship and strength of God's Holy Spirit.

Choosing life is seeking to live more fully, enabling those around you to flourish.

Choosing life is choosing to say yes to the life that Jesus offers.

What does it mean for you to choose life today and for the New Year?

READ John 10.7-10

New Year's Day

Step Out

A new year begins. Perhaps it offers new opportunities and possibilities. It certainly offers the chance to live differently even within realities that don't change.

Your Christmas journey began with a step, and continues in just the same way. As you have reflected over these last few days, what are the steps you need to take today to turn intentions into reality?

It might be that you realise you need to change something you do or an attitude you have. You may have seen that you need to put something right, go and talk to someone or explore something further.

> *When Jesus turned and saw them following, he said to them, 'What are you looking for?' They said to him, 'Rabbi' (which translated means Teacher), 'where are you staying?' He said to them, 'Come and see.'*

You might simply realise that this year needs to be lived differently, at a different pace, with space for reflection and prayer and with a desire to see God in your life.

You might also have seen that the heart of that change is Jesus Christ, born in Bethlehem, whose words and life speak to us today. By his Holy Spirit, he lives in us today and walks alongside us. #GodWithUs always.

When Jesus called the first disciples to follow him, he didn't give them a manual or a pep talk, he simply said, 'Come and see.' Step out, walk with Jesus and see what happens.

What's your first step today to live differently?

READ John 1.36-39

Going Further

We hope that you have enjoyed the journey of the last few days. It doesn't stop here. There are many ways in which you can go further.

Explore more about Jesus and the Christian life

- For further daily reflections visit **www.soulfood.me** and take a look at the menu. LifeSteps would be a good choice.
- To find out more about the life of Jesus and his relevance for today visit **www.rejesus.co.uk**
- To find help and encouragement in daily prayer visit the Church of England website **www.churchofengland.org** where you can access daily services or download the free **Daily Prayer app**.

Meet with others to discuss and learn together

- Many churches run short courses such as *Alpha* and *Pilgrim*. They are a great place to ask questions and find some answers. Have a look at **www.alpha.org/try** or **www.pilgrimcourse.org**
- Other churches run regular discussion groups in pubs or over lunch, or offer events during the week where you can meet others and explore worship, prayer and faith such as *Messy Church*.

In the end the best way to go further on your Christmas journey is by finding a church in which you feel at home and in which you can thrive.

Find a church and get involved

- There's a church for you: it might be near where you live or close to where you work. Find a place where you can experience the peace and joy of God's presence.
- Have a look at **www.achurchnearyou.com** to discover more or ask a friend about a church they might know of or belong to.
- A great way to grow in faith is to get involved. It's certainly not just about going to a Sunday service. Many churches would love your help, for example, with the Night Shelters or Food Banks they run.

And finally, it's worth remembering that churches are not full of experts. When it comes to faith we are all on a journey, all still learning and discovering more.

Published 2017 by Church House Publishing
www.chpublishing.co.uk

Church House, Great Smith Street, London SW1P 3AZ

Single ISBN 978 1 78140 066 1
Pk 10 ISBN 978 1 78140 069 2
Pk 50 ISBN 978 1 78140 070 8

Written by John Kiddle

The opinions expressed in this book are those of the author.

Design by www.penguinboy.net

Printed in the UK by Ashford Colour Press

A catalogue record for this publication is available from the British Library

Acknowledgements

Renewal & Reform

The #GodWithUs Christmas project is part of the Church of England's Renewal
and Reform programme, aimed at helping us become a growing Church for all
people and for all places. Find out more about #GodWithUs and join in online at
www.churchofengland.org/Christmas

Your Christmas Journey has been developed in association with soul[food].

soul[food] is an initiative which offers people the opportunity to explore a variety of
themes of life and faith in bite-sized thoughts sent straight to a phone or inbox. It is
based at the Church of England Diocese of Birmingham. To find out more and sign
up, visit soulfood.me

Bible readings are taken from *The New Revised Standard Version (Anglicized Edition)*,
copyright 1989, 1995 by the Division of Christian Education of the National Council of
the Churches of Christ in the United States of America. All rights reserved.